TEAR TALK

TEAR TALK
A 90 DAY GUIDE TO HEALING THROUGH JOURNALING

MASHANI ALLEN

Copyright ©2018 by MaShani Allen

Revised and Redistributed in ©2021

Unless otherwise indicated, all Scripture quotations are taken from the King James (KJV) of the Bible.

Scriptures taken from the Holy Bible, New International Version®, NIV®. Copyright © 1973, 1978, 1984, 2011 by Biblica, Inc.™ Used by permission of Zondervan. www.zondervan.com

The "NIV" and "New International Version" are trademarks registered in the United States Patent and Trademark Office by Biblica, Inc.™

Scripture taken from the Contemporary English Version © 1991, 1992, 1995 by American Bible Society.

Used by Permission.

Cover Design: MaShani Allen

Author Photo: J'Nae Antoinette Photography

Tear Talk A 90-Day Guide to Healing through Journaling Visit the author's website at www.MaShaniAllen.com Library of Congress Cataloging-in-Publication Data:

An application to register this book for cataloging has been submitted to the Library of Congress.

All rights reserved. No part of this publication may be reproduced, stored in a retrieval system, or transmitted in any form or by any means—electronic, mechanical, digital, photocopy, recording, or any other— except for brief quotations in printed reviews, without the prior permission of the publisher.

While the author has made every effort to provide accurate Internet addresses at the time of publication, neither the publisher nor the author assumes any responsibility for errors or for changes that occur after publication.

First edition

Printed in the United States of America

Connect with MaShani and join her mailing list at

www.MaShaniAllen.com

FB @MaShaniAllenAuthor

IG @MaShani Allen

Tear Talk
I've been
confined
I've been held
back,
When my mission is to leak and flow while you think, write and speak.
I've been
avoided,
I've been
denied,
I've wanted to run but instead, I was forced to go and hide.
I've been
misunderstood,
I've been made to bring
shame,
When my role is to help heal the soul and release the blame.
Please let me flow,
It will help you heal and grow.
Please let me release,
It will bring so much joy and peace.
Please let me go,
It will help the true you shine and glow.
@MaShani Allen

INTRODUCTION

Often when we mention healing, people shrink back, wanting to avoid the unavoidable. One of the best ways to receive healing is through the expression of your own thoughts. Many of us need to unpack our brains. We have so many thoughts swirling in our heads with no place for release. A journal is that place. Don't fear the pen. Many times when you find or discover your pen, you also discover your voice. Your pen and paper don't judge you. You won't see a strange facial expression or hear a rebuttal. You will just see words written on a page or hear the sound of a keyboard. The brain is the ultimate computer full of data consisting of experiences, dreams, thoughts, opinions, and much more. As life happens, it can become full, and some things can be suppressed. All doesn't have to be negative, but not being able to get it out can be overwhelming. Also, sometimes it can be difficult to remember. Journaling is a remedy. Freedom of expression is granted. Not sure where to start? A writing prompt will get you started so that you can flow.

In this book, you will be provided with 90 prompts meant to enable you to feel comfortable with expressing your thoughts. You can use these prompts in any order. However, all prompts should be completed. I recommend setting aside at least 20-30 minutes daily to answer a question and pen your correlating thoughts. Before you jump to the questions, I would like to give you a brief understanding of unlocking your heart. When it comes to change, our society focuses on the outer person. This focus makes the concept of inner healing seemingly difficult to understand but is rather simple. Let me give you an example. Think of

TEAR TALK: A 90 DAY GUIDE TO HEALING THROUGH JOURNALING

a car. Whether you are a passenger or driver, you understand that a car does not operate simply by putting the key in the ignition. Underneath the hood, there is an engine, valves, oil, and many other parts that work together. When the car shows signs of difficulty starting, the mechanic will check multiple parts to diagnose the issue. This is what you will be doing with your journal and the questions provided.

As I was preparing for *Tear Talk*, I thought of the challenges each person might face. Many times crying is frowned upon, and questions are avoided to shy away from true emotions. We are discouraged from being able to express our true and raw feelings. This inadvertently can place an unknown lock on our hearts. Tears are left unable to speak or be released. Emotions can have a negative outlook when expressed, which causes many to hide, deny or reject their feelings. Tears are important, and crying is healthy.

> *You have kept record of my days of wandering. You have stored my tears in your bottle and counted each of them.*
> Ps 56:8 <u>CEV</u>

Though people may not understand your tears, they are precious to God. My hope with this book is that you would let your tears flow and let your tears speak.

A question can be the most effective way to bridge that gap, but they are often shunned or ignored. The greatest challenge, I believe, is facing the questions that will bring healing. Somewhere between childhood and adulthood, we learn to devalue asking questions. Some can view questions as weapons when in actuality, they are keys. We get to the point where we don't want to be asked questions out of fear of the answer. But there is a power that comes with asking questions. Questions are not to be avoided. Personally, in the past few weeks, a lot of questions have been coming to mind. They are not surface questions; they are deep questions. Questions that make me have to look deep within myself. They are challenging but unavoidable if I want to grow.

Just as you are using this book to learn and receive inner healing, God will bring people into your life to ask you deep questions to make you dig below the surface and challenge you. Questions like: "Where did you get that mindset from?" "Where did you get that thought process from?" "When did that mental stronghold begin?" These questions will point you toward the truth and highlight what doesn't line up with where you're going. You may even be wondering, 'Why have I not been able to get the release that I know is coming to me?' You probably have some hard questions to answer.

We are going back to the example of the car. Our heart is like the engine to everything we do. The way we respond to situations allows us to see our character, which reflects our heart.

Ezekiel 36:26 says:

> *"And I will give you a new heart, and I will put a new spirit in you. I will take out your stony, stubborn heart and give you a tender, responsive heart."*

This scripture shows us the heart can have different attributes. All hearts aren't the same. The hearts are categorized as "stony" or "stubborn," which aren't positive attributes. Yet, the blessing is these conditions can change. These stony and stubborn hearts are locked. Remember I said you would be unlocking your healing. This process begins with your heart. Still, before you can unlock it, you will need to discover how your heart is locked. There may be more than one way. Many of us experienced a locking in our hearts through hurt, evil actions toward us, abandonment, rejection, trauma, and shame, to name a few. Other ways our hearts can be locked are through disappointment, anger, and resentment. When the chambers of our heart become locked, it causes us not fully to be who God originally intended us to be. Like the growth happening on a farm, there is more going on beneath the surface than above. Much of who you are isn't based on what you look like or act like, but on what is going on inside of you.

Proverbs 4:23 tells us,

TEAR TALK: A 90 DAY GUIDE TO HEALING THROUGH JOURNALING

"Above all else, guard your heart, for everything you do flows from it."

Sadly, many of us are never taught how to guard a heart. We don't understand the difference between guarding and locking. When something is locked, there is typically a limitation or no access. When you have the following things in your heart, you limit love, and your true personality is hindered. These deep-seated emotions, when undealt with, act as a gate or barrier to the true you being revealed.

Emotions that lock (when not addressed):

- Anger – a strong feeling of annoyance, displeasure, or hostility
- Unforgiveness – not willing to forgive other people
- Bitterness – causing painful emotions: felt or experienced in a strong and unpleasant way: angry and unhappy because of unfair treatment
- Insecurity – not confident about yourself or your ability to do things well: nervous and uncomfortable: not certain to continue or be successful for a long time: not locked or well protected
- Jealousy – an unhappy or angry feeling of wanting to have what someone else has
- Envy – painful or resentful awareness of an advantage enjoyed by another joined with a desire to possess the same advantage

But the greatest barrier is

- FEAR – to be afraid of (something or someone): to expect or worry about (something bad or unpleasant): to be afraid and worried

Could you relate to any of these? You may have a few that were highlighted to you. Now that you can see how we can become locked, I would like to share a biblical story of a woman who became unlocked. This story illustrates a few keys we can use in our own lives to be unlocked.

In John 4, we see an encounter between Jesus and a woman at a well. In this powerful story, we learn that she was no ordinary woman but a woman of controversy. She'd been married at least five times, and it's unclear exactly how many men she had been with. Many of us would not understand why Jesus would choose such a woman to break the strongholds of culture, race, and religion. We can't see the keys used that will help in our unlocking. Yet, the unlocking for this woman would not have been possible without one question and the woman's ability, to be honest.

"At this, Jesus said to her, Go, call your husband and come back here. The woman answered I have no husband. Jesus said to her, You have spoken truly in saying, I have no husband. For you have had five husbands, and the man you are now living with is not your husband. In this, you have spoken truly."

-- John 4:16-18

Honesty is the greatest key to unlocking your inner healing. The woman probably felt relieved to finally, freely tell the truth. She may have wanted to change her life for a while but didn't know-how. She probably wanted a fresh start but didn't know where to go. Jesus, a stranger, asked her a question, which began her quest for freedom. When Jesus met the woman at the well, she was open and receptive to him.

Most importantly, she was honest with herself first, then with Jesus. She listened to Him recite her past. She did not lie when the truth about her was revealed. Jesus recalled the past, not to expose the woman but to acknowledge her honesty.

We must do the same. When the truth about where we are and where we have been surfaces, we must take ownership. Lying will perpetuate a vicious cycle of sin. Being honest will set us free. The questions Jesus posed went beneath the surface. (Taken from author's book, *The Beauty of Holiness: A Makeover From The Inside Out*). Some of us are praised for external changes we have made, but internally we are crying out for someone to hear our heart. Jesus is waiting patiently to dig beneath the surface and heal our brokenness. Only then can we truly enjoy freedom. Below are other elements needed to unlock your healing.

Keys to Unlock:

- Forgiveness
- Faith
- Word of God – Isaiah 58:11, John 4:14
- Prayer

Forgiveness is more about you than the person who wronged you. When forgiveness is stuck in your soul, you will most likely become suspicious, resentful, and fearful. It's about what you become on the inside when you don't let go of the hurt.

As you unlock your healing, the parts of your heart that have been locked will transform. Instead of being "stony" or "stubborn," these parts will be "tender" and "responsive." Your new heart will also show new characteristics. The tenderness will show through these attributes, which you will receive:

- Wisdom – the soundness of an action or decision with regard to the application of experience, knowledge, and good judgment.
- Humility – the quality or state of not thinking you are better than other people
- Grace – a controlled, polite, and pleasant way of behaving
- Joy – the emotion evoked by well-being, success, or good fortune or by the prospect of possessing what one desires
- Peace – freedom from disquieting or oppressive thoughts or emotions, harmony in personal relations

When we look at the woman at the well in John 4, a conversation with Jesus brought such liberation to her and not only to her but even to a town of people who had absolutely rejected her. She was considered an outcast, but after talking with Jesus, the woman ran back to the town and told everyone. In one conversation, she was healed, delivered, and set free. In one conversation, she was given hope, peace, and encouragement. In one conversation, her burdens were lifted, and the pain was replaced with joy. The woman was so excited that she went to the same people who had talked about her, rejected her, and made her feel ashamed; she didn't care about the possible backlash. She was so liberated it did not matter. Her testimony was so strong and powerful that others came looking for Jesus. This was all due to one dialogue. This was due to questions and honest answers. Could you imagine the kind of freedom that causes you to share your healing with the very ones who caused your heart to be locked? This kind of healing can be yours. My admonishment to you is this: don't avoid the questions.

You can't overcome what you don't confront. You can't get free from what you won't admit. There are pains, hurt, and emotions that cannot go with you into the future God is taking you to. Don't avoid the hard questions. Don't avoid the deep questions. When you face the questions, don't be quick to give an answer and feel as though that's the final answer. To overcome your thought process, you may have to address the question multiple times. This may be a thought process God doesn't want you to have anymore.

If we are honest, many of our thoughts don't line up with scripture. They are just thought processes we've had for years. Then the word of God comes to confront us. I literally had a friend confront me and ask, "where did you get that thought from? Why are you thinking that way?" At the moment, I personally was displeased over the questioning, but it was needful. The more I thought about it, the more I realized that it didn't line up with what God was saying and what God has been speaking regarding my future.

Don't be afraid of questions or the answers that will come as you write. Questions bring revelation. Questions bring insight. Questions bring clarity. Questions bring liberty. Questions bring freedom. Questions bring truth. Silence is the loudest scream. Many are emotionally and internally screaming because they aren't answering the questions that will bring healing. They are silent on the outside while screaming on the inside. If this is you, I want you to know that you shouldn't be screaming on the inside. There's a level of freedom that will come if you answer the hard questions.

My background in journalism and counseling has made me comfortable with questions. I ask questions all the time. But the absence of fear towards facing hard questions and answering with honesty isn't just for me. It took time and consistency to be comfortable with questions. I cannot emphasize this enough… do not be afraid of the questions. Truth doesn't always feel good, but it's necessary and needful. Allow truth to rise as you answer the questions and set aside denial. When Jesus told the woman at the well to get her husband, he caused her to confront her situation with the truth. She could have used denial to cover up that she did not have a husband, but she didn't. When we aren't honest, we limit what He (Jesus) can do in our lives.

Answering hard questions doesn't just unlock our inner healing. When we unlock healing, we obtain a new heart, new characteristics, a new perspective, which draws in new relationships. Certain relationships can't come into your life until you answer the hard questions because there are parts of your past you can't take into new friendships. Different emotional wounds you definitely don't want to into your marriage. These deep-seated emotions can hinder your ministry. Even a new job can be impacted by what is not unlocked.

There must be a shifting in mindsets if we really want to be liberated and fully unlocked. Questions show you what's on the inside of you, good or bad. The wonderful thing is nothing is permanent. You can work on the bad. You can talk about what locked you and talk through mindsets so that you can be liberated. When those hard questions are being posed, you can journal your response. Just getting it out will bring a level of healing and liberty. Being able to get it out will allow Him to the barriers to the real you. That's what He came to do to heal and to deliver. The process of your healing will involve mindsets being shifted and thought processes being changed. You can't, and shouldn't want to, rush your process.

Much of what needs to be unlocked go deeper than we care to admit and deeper than some of us really want to find out. The deeper He goes, the more He challenges me. But If He's going that deep and He's really challenging me, then He must be doing this because He knows much where I'm going. That is how you have to look at it. When the questions and answers become challenging, think: "I want my promise too much! I want to get completely unlocked and be ready for all He has for me." Now that you have an understanding of the keys, you are ready to unlock your healing. The following is a list of 90 prompts to use in the coming days to journal your way to even deeper healing. Remember, you can't rush the process, but you should face each question to get the most from what God has for you. Choose a prompt taking 20-30 minutes minimum to sit, think, write, and respond. There is no right or wrong way to respond. You may find that with a few of these, your response will be more creative, and others will be more of the style of a diary.

A 90 DAY

GUIDE TO

HEALING

DAY 1

Read Psalms 91. How does the passage make you feel? Are there any instances you felt you were not protected?

_____

_____

_____

_____

_____

_____

_____

_____

_____

_____

_____

_____

_____

_____

TEAR TALK: A 90 DAY GUIDE TO HEALING THROUGH JOURNALING

DAY 2

Read Psalms 23. Rewrite and replace "my" with your name. How does that make you feel? What does being cared for mean to you? Is there anything from the passage you feel you have been missing or not allowing the Lord to do in your life?

TEAR TALK: A 90 DAY GUIDE TO HEALING THROUGH JOURNALING

DAY 3

Character prompt-(Read the story of David and Goliath in 1 Samuel 17. Who or what is your Goliath? [Something or someone that challenges you]

_____

_____

_____

_____

_____

_____

_____

_____

_____

_____

_____

_____

TEAR TALK: A 90 DAY GUIDE TO HEALING THROUGH JOURNALING

DAY 4

Character prompt- What has been your furnace? [Share an experience where you felt like you were in a fiery trial? How long was it? How did it end?]

_____

_____

_____

_____

_____

_____

_____

_____

_____

_____

_____

_____

_____

_____

TEAR TALK: A 90 DAY GUIDE TO HEALING THROUGH JOURNALING

DAY 5

Character prompt- Read Luke 22. Do you have a Judas? If so, who is it?

_____

_____

_____

_____

_____

_____

_____

_____

_____

_____

_____

_____

_____

_____

TEAR TALK: A 90 DAY GUIDE TO HEALING THROUGH JOURNALING

DAY 6

Music has a way of speaking to us. Take your favorite album and each day write based on a song title and lyrics.

TEAR TALK: A 90 DAY GUIDE TO HEALING THROUGH JOURNALING

$\mathcal{D}$AY 7

Dear God……[write a heartfelt letter to God]

TEAR TALK: A 90 DAY GUIDE TO HEALING THROUGH JOURNALING

$\mathscr{D}$AY 8

Watch the Disney movie Moana or Lion King and write any thoughts or insight you receive. [Which character do you relate to the most? Why?]

TEAR TALK: A 90 DAY GUIDE TO HEALING THROUGH JOURNALING

DAY 9

If you could write a letter to the younger you what would you say?

_____
_____
_____
_____
_____
_____
_____
_____
_____
_____
_____
_____
_____
_____

TEAR TALK: A 90 DAY GUIDE TO HEALING THROUGH JOURNALING

DAY 10

If you could write a letter to your role model, what would you say?

_____
_____
_____
_____
_____
_____
_____
_____
_____
_____
_____
_____
_____
_____
_____

TEAR TALK: A 90 DAY GUIDE TO HEALING THROUGH JOURNALING

DAY 11

Who was your favorite teacher, and why?

TEAR TALK: A 90 DAY GUIDE TO HEALING THROUGH JOURNALING

DAY 12

What is your favorite sermon, and why?

TEAR TALK: A 90 DAY GUIDE TO HEALING THROUGH JOURNALING

DAY 13

What is the best speech you've heard and why?

TEAR TALK: A 90 DAY GUIDE TO HEALING THROUGH JOURNALING

DAY 14

What is your favorite book, and why?

TEAR TALK: A 90 DAY GUIDE TO HEALING THROUGH JOURNALING

DAY 15

If you could describe yourself as a biblical character, who would it be and why?

_____
_____
_____
_____
_____
_____
_____
_____
_____
_____
_____
_____
_____
_____

TEAR TALK: A 90 DAY GUIDE TO HEALING THROUGH JOURNALING

DAY 16

What is the best dream you ever had?

_____
_____
_____
_____
_____
_____
_____
_____
_____
_____
_____
_____
_____
_____

TEAR TALK: A 90 DAY GUIDE TO HEALING THROUGH JOURNALING

$\mathcal{D}$AY 17

What is your favorite childhood memory? [Do you have one? If you don't, why not?]

_____
_____
_____
_____
_____
_____
_____
_____
_____
_____
_____
_____
_____
_____

TEAR TALK: A 90 DAY GUIDE TO HEALING THROUGH JOURNALING

DAY 18

What is an apology that you need to give that you haven't?

_____
_____
_____
_____
_____
_____
_____
_____
_____
_____
_____
_____
_____
_____

TEAR TALK: A 90 DAY GUIDE TO HEALING THROUGH JOURNALING

DAY 19

What is your most painful memory?

TEAR TALK: A 90 DAY GUIDE TO HEALING THROUGH JOURNALING

DAY 20

Do you embrace that you are great? If so, how? If not, why not?

_____
_____
_____
_____
_____
_____
_____
_____
_____
_____
_____
_____
_____
_____

TEAR TALK: A 90 DAY GUIDE TO HEALING THROUGH JOURNALING

DAY 21

What is your relationship like with your parents? Write what you would want to say to your parents that you've never been able to say.

_____

_____

_____

_____

_____

_____

_____

_____

_____

_____

_____

_____

_____

_____

TEAR TALK: A 90 DAY GUIDE TO HEALING THROUGH JOURNALING

DAY 22

What is your relationship with your siblings or family members? If you could say something to your siblings or family members that you've never shared, what would it be?

_____

_____

_____

_____

_____

_____

_____

_____

_____

_____

_____

_____

TEAR TALK: A 90 DAY GUIDE TO HEALING THROUGH JOURNALING

DAY 23

Who, what, where, when, and why?

TEAR TALK: A 90 DAY GUIDE TO HEALING THROUGH JOURNALING

DAY 24

What is your biggest dream?

TEAR TALK: A 90 DAY GUIDE TO HEALING THROUGH JOURNALING

DAY 25

What is your greatest fear?

TEAR TALK: A 90 DAY GUIDE TO HEALING THROUGH JOURNALING

DAY 26

What is your deepest secret?

TEAR TALK: A 90 DAY GUIDE TO HEALING THROUGH JOURNALING

DAY 27

What is your greatest regret?

TEAR TALK: A 90 DAY GUIDE TO HEALING THROUGH JOURNALING

$\mathcal{D}$AY 28

What was your greatest loss?

TEAR TALK: A 90 DAY GUIDE TO HEALING THROUGH JOURNALING

DAY 29

What is your greatest blessing?

TEAR TALK: A 90 DAY GUIDE TO HEALING THROUGH JOURNALING

DAY 30

Do you feel that you are in purpose? Why or Why not?

___

TEAR TALK: A 90 DAY GUIDE TO HEALING THROUGH JOURNALING

DAY 31

If you could be anything, what would it be and why?

TEAR TALK: A 90 DAY GUIDE TO HEALING THROUGH JOURNALING

DAY 32

What is your greatest shame?

TEAR TALK: A 90 DAY GUIDE TO HEALING THROUGH JOURNALING

DAY 33

What has been your biggest challenge in life?

_____
_____
_____
_____
_____
_____
_____
_____
_____
_____
_____
_____
_____
_____

TEAR TALK: A 90 DAY GUIDE TO HEALING THROUGH JOURNALING

DAY 34

What has been your greatest victory?

TEAR TALK: A 90 DAY GUIDE TO HEALING THROUGH JOURNALING

Day 35

What is your testimony?

TEAR TALK: A 90 DAY GUIDE TO HEALING THROUGH JOURNALING

DAY 36

Do you have a best friend? What makes that friendship different from others? If no, is there a reason you don't?

_____

_____

_____

_____

_____

_____

_____

_____

_____

_____

_____

_____

_____

TEAR TALK: A 90 DAY GUIDE TO HEALING THROUGH JOURNALING

DAY 37

What is your definition of forgiveness?

TEAR TALK: A 90 DAY GUIDE TO HEALING THROUGH JOURNALING

DAY 38

How would you describe yourself? [Imagine yourself introducing two people who are strangers to one another. One of the people is you. How would you describe yourself? Does the dialogue change based on who you are introducing yourself to?]

TEAR TALK: A 90 DAY GUIDE TO HEALING THROUGH JOURNALING

Day 39

How did your heart get locked?

TEAR TALK: A 90 DAY GUIDE TO HEALING THROUGH JOURNALING

DAY 40

What keys were used to keep your heart locked?

_____
_____
_____
_____
_____
_____
_____
_____
_____
_____
_____
_____
_____
_____
_____
_____
_____

TEAR TALK: A 90 DAY GUIDE TO HEALING THROUGH JOURNALING

DAY 41

What keys can you use to unlock your heart?

_____
_____
_____
_____
_____
_____
_____
_____
_____
_____
_____
_____
_____
_____
_____

TEAR TALK: A 90 DAY GUIDE TO HEALING THROUGH JOURNALING

DAY 42

What can having a locked heart hinder? [How have you been hindered by having a locked heart?]

_____
_____
_____
_____
_____
_____
_____
_____
_____
_____
_____
_____
_____
_____

TEAR TALK: A 90 DAY GUIDE TO HEALING THROUGH JOURNALING

$\mathcal{D}$AY 43

Why do people fear dealing with a locked heart? [What are you most afraid of when it comes to unlocking your heart?]

TEAR TALK: A 90 DAY GUIDE TO HEALING THROUGH JOURNALING

DAY 44

Why do we ignore our real feelings? [What emotions have you been ignoring? Write about one incident and what you were feeling. Can you identify the emotion?]

_____
_____
_____
_____
_____
_____
_____
_____
_____
_____
_____
_____

TEAR TALK: A 90 DAY GUIDE TO HEALING THROUGH JOURNALING

DAY 45

How much have words and people's thoughts and opinions influenced you?

TEAR TALK: A 90 DAY GUIDE TO HEALING THROUGH JOURNALING

DAY 46

How do you guard your heart?

TEAR TALK: A 90 DAY GUIDE TO HEALING THROUGH JOURNALING

DAY 47

Should healing come easy?

TEAR TALK: A 90 DAY GUIDE TO HEALING THROUGH JOURNALING

DAY 48

How do you forgive?

TEAR TALK: A 90 DAY GUIDE TO HEALING THROUGH JOURNALING

DAY 49

Can we really be free from childhood wounds? [Write about one instance from your childhood that you are still holding onto the pain. What would letting go of the pain, and trusting Jesus mean for you?]

TEAR TALK: A 90 DAY GUIDE TO HEALING THROUGH JOURNALING

DAY 50

Write a letter to your future self, the self you expect to meet after the 90 prompts are finished. Share what you expect or how you see yourself. Keep this letter and read it on the last day.

_____
_____
_____
_____
_____
_____
_____
_____
_____
_____
_____
_____
_____
_____

TEAR TALK: A 90 DAY GUIDE TO HEALING THROUGH JOURNALING

DAY 51

Are you worth your healing? Do you believe you are valuable enough to be made whole?

TEAR TALK: A 90 DAY GUIDE TO HEALING THROUGH JOURNALING

DAY 52

Imagine you are the woman at the well. Rewrite the dialogue between you and Jesus.

TEAR TALK: A 90 DAY GUIDE TO HEALING THROUGH JOURNALING

DAY 53

Ask Jesus to reveal your heart to you. How does it look? Describe it below. Draw a visual if you can.

TEAR TALK: A 90 DAY GUIDE TO HEALING THROUGH JOURNALING

DAY 54

(Creative prompt) Write a short story using this sentence in any section you choose. "Distracted by the pain, I didn't hear the door lock until it was too late."

TEAR TALK: A 90 DAY GUIDE TO HEALING THROUGH JOURNALING

DAY 55

(Creative prompt) Write a story or poem using this sentence: "My heart has new feeling because of deeper healing, I never thought I'd need."

TEAR TALK: A 90 DAY GUIDE TO HEALING THROUGH JOURNALING

DAY 56

Finish this statement: "I never knew real love until…"

TEAR TALK: A 90 DAY GUIDE TO HEALING THROUGH JOURNALING

Day 57

Finish this statement: "An unlocked heart feels like..."

TEAR TALK: A 90 DAY GUIDE TO HEALING THROUGH JOURNALING

DAY 58

Finish this sentence: "The first person I want to tell about my healing is _____." Write them a letter.

TEAR TALK: A 90 DAY GUIDE TO HEALING THROUGH JOURNALING

DAY 59

Write out John 3:16. What does this mean to you? How do you describe that love?

TEAR TALK: A 90 DAY GUIDE TO HEALING THROUGH JOURNALING

DAY 60

How will you keep your heart from being locked again?

TEAR TALK: A 90 DAY GUIDE TO HEALING THROUGH JOURNALING

DAY 61

Is trust given or earned? How do you trust?

_____
_____
_____
_____
_____
_____
_____
_____
_____
_____
_____
_____
_____
_____
_____

TEAR TALK: A 90 DAY GUIDE TO HEALING THROUGH JOURNALING

DAY 62

If you could measure grace, how much do you have for others? How much do you have for yourself?

TEAR TALK: A 90 DAY GUIDE TO HEALING THROUGH JOURNALING

DAY 63

What would happen if others saw you fail?

TEAR TALK: A 90 DAY GUIDE TO HEALING THROUGH JOURNALING

DAY 64

When are you most happy? Could you have joy without anything happening to or for you?

TEAR TALK: A 90 DAY GUIDE TO HEALING THROUGH JOURNALING

DAY 65

Do you like spending large amounts of time alone? Why or why not?

TEAR TALK: A 90 DAY GUIDE TO HEALING THROUGH JOURNALING

DAY 66

Imagine you are in a room filled with strangers for an important event honoring you. Write about the experience. (Would you wait for people to come to you or go to them? Describe the people. What would you talk about?)

TEAR TALK: A 90 DAY GUIDE TO HEALING THROUGH JOURNALING

DAY 67

If you could be any animal which one and why? What are the attributes of that animal?

TEAR TALK: A 90 DAY GUIDE TO HEALING THROUGH JOURNALING

DAY 68

What is your definition of success? Have you arrived at success?

TEAR TALK: A 90 DAY GUIDE TO HEALING THROUGH JOURNALING

DAY 69

What is your favorite scripture, and why?

TEAR TALK: A 90 DAY GUIDE TO HEALING THROUGH JOURNALING

DAY 70

What book or movie changed your life or had a profound impact. Be as detailed as possible when writing the account.

TEAR TALK: A 90 DAY GUIDE TO HEALING THROUGH JOURNALING

DAY 71

From the book by Gary Chapman, The Five Love Languages- what is your love language? Do you receive love the way you desire?

TEAR TALK: A 90 DAY GUIDE TO HEALING THROUGH JOURNALING

DAY 72

What is your most memorable moment in high school?

___
___
___
___
___
___
___
___
___
___
___
___
___

TEAR TALK: A 90 DAY GUIDE TO HEALING THROUGH JOURNALING

DAY 73

If you were chosen to be in a movie or a television program which film or show would you choose and why?

TEAR TALK: A 90 DAY GUIDE TO HEALING THROUGH JOURNALING

DAY 74

What has been your greatest achievement in life?

TEAR TALK: A 90 DAY GUIDE TO HEALING THROUGH JOURNALING

Day 75

If you were a superhero, who would you be and why?

TEAR TALK: A 90 DAY GUIDE TO HEALING THROUGH JOURNALING

DAY 76

Read Jeremiah 29:11. Write it out and replace "you" with your name. Do you know any of the plans? Do you believe the plans?

_____

_____

_____

_____

_____

_____

_____

_____

_____

_____

_____

_____

_____

_____

TEAR TALK: A 90 DAY GUIDE TO HEALING THROUGH JOURNALING

DAY 77

Share an opportunity that you missed if given a second chance; what would you do differently?

_____
_____
_____
_____
_____
_____
_____
_____
_____
_____
_____
_____
_____
_____

TEAR TALK: A 90 DAY GUIDE TO HEALING THROUGH JOURNALING

DAY 78

What are your gifts and strengths? How do you use them?

TEAR TALK: A 90 DAY GUIDE TO HEALING THROUGH JOURNALING

DAY 79

How do you handle criticism and critique?

TEAR TALK: A 90 DAY GUIDE TO HEALING THROUGH JOURNALING

DAY 80

What areas in your life do you need to grow and develop? What process have you put in place to monitor the growth?

TEAR TALK: A 90 DAY GUIDE TO HEALING THROUGH JOURNALING

DAY 81

Who are your greatest cheerleaders in life? Write a letter of appreciation to them.

TEAR TALK: A 90 DAY GUIDE TO HEALING THROUGH JOURNALING

DAY 82

Write your personal mission and mandate in life.

TEAR TALK: A 90 DAY GUIDE TO HEALING THROUGH JOURNALING

DAY 83

If you were alone on an island and only two people could be with you, who would you choose and why?

TEAR TALK: A 90 DAY GUIDE TO HEALING THROUGH JOURNALING

DAY 84

If you could ask one question to your favorite celebrity (actor, singer, speaker, etc.), what would it be?

TEAR TALK: A 90 DAY GUIDE TO HEALING THROUGH JOURNALING

DAY 85

Write a letter of inspiration to your children, grandchildren, nieces, or nephews.

TEAR TALK: A 90 DAY GUIDE TO HEALING THROUGH JOURNALING

DAY 86

What are your thoughts on legacy?

_____

_____

_____

_____

_____

_____

_____

_____

_____

_____

_____

_____

_____

_____

TEAR TALK: A 90 DAY GUIDE TO HEALING THROUGH JOURNALING

DAY 87

If there were a news story written about your life, what would you like it to say?

TEAR TALK: A 90 DAY GUIDE TO HEALING THROUGH JOURNALING

DAY 88

Take 10 mins to write down all the questions you have for God. [Take 10 mins to allow Him to answer]

TEAR TALK: A 90 DAY GUIDE TO HEALING THROUGH JOURNALING

DAY 89

If you could summarize your life in one word, what would it be? Now look that word up in the dictionary and write the definition.

_____

_____

_____

_____

_____

_____

_____

_____

_____

_____

_____

_____

_____

_____

TEAR TALK: A 90 DAY GUIDE TO HEALING THROUGH JOURNALING

DAY 90

What is your definition of unique? How do you apply that to yourself?

# TEAR TALK: A 90 DAY GUIDE TO HEALING THROUGH JOURNALING

I want to personally thank you for reading Tear Talk A 90-Day Guide to Healing through Journaling. I pray that this brought a new measure of understanding to your identity and closure to deep wounds and hurts. Don't let this be the last time you pick up your pen. Continue to write, continue to heal, continue to discover. Always remember there is Power in the Pen.

Connect with me www.MaShaniAllen.com

FB @MaShaniAllenAuthor

IG @MaShani Allen

Twitter @MaShani Allen

www.ingramcontent.com/pod-product-compliance
Lightning Source LLC
Chambersburg PA
CBHW051432290426
44109CB00016B/1525